Expropriation of the Mind Without Compensation

The New Revolution Isn't on the Streets; It's in the Mind.

Hardpiece Kabala

HARDPIECE KABALA

About the author

Kabala Hardpiece

Kabala Hardpiece is the founder and leader of the Free-Minded/Peuple Libre organisation, a pan-African social and religious organisation based in South Africa. For more information, visit www.peuplelibre.org

Acknowledgments

To my wife Allegresse for her encouragement for me to write the book and to the leading team of the Free-Minded/Peuple Libre organisation for the suggestions and advice that have made this work possible. To Etana and Asantewaa.

Introduction

You are about to discover one of the powerful tools for life transformation. Your life will function differently from the moment you read this book and set new principles of life based on your understanding of the truths revealed in this book. The different chapters are written for one goal - liberating the mind. However, liberation requires a deep understanding of yourself and knowledge of the truth in different aspects: spiritual, psychological and physical about you, and the truth about everything in the universe. This book is written exclusively for African people who live daily with the burning hope of change in their lives particularly and change in the continent generally. It is also written for religious people, specifically for Christians, as the major religion in Africa, to understand the difference between faith and knowledge, religion and spirituality. This will allow them to always act in the appropriate manner according to time, context and circumstances and to truly live as the light and the salt of the world.

Life is not a gift; it is an assignment. Once you understand this principle, you are on the right path for changing your life. Nobody is indebted for a gift received, but we are accountable for life. If you don't judge yourself, the world will judge you. If you think your life is a gift you have no problems to solve and you don't have responsibilities. You were born without language, culture, religion, friends and knowledge – you were born with a mission. Anything you have and know today, whether it is language, religion, culture, a name or knowledge, are things people you have found in this world gave to you. People gave you a name, culture, languages, religion and knowledge, but they have given them to you without knowing you or your real mission on Earth. Any person can give you something for different reasons, mainly because they believe it is something you need, or they want you to make use of what they have given you to produce the results appropriate to their opinions. Yet, what you need always depends on the nature of your mission. That mission remains unknown until you discover and disclose it. Therefore, your first priority in life is to discover your mission, then you can use everything people give you to accomplish it. Our lives today are shaped and dictated by the cultures received from people we found, but if these cultures lead us to become unproductive people controlled by fear, or people who are hateful of other people for who they are and what they believe, then we are far from accomplishing our mission. Instead, it is like we are remote controlled by people who systematically install in us cultures that produce the results they want. We were born without fear, except for the fear babes have of noise and falling. We were not born hateful of other people, but we have received and maybe accepted a lot of cultures and beliefs that darken our minds. The only time anything can help you is when you can use it to accomplish your mission. Nothing else will give meaning to your life; only you can make something meaningful of your life. Hence, discover why you have life and learn what to do with what falls into your hands. In reading this book you will learn to stop being used and know how to meaningfully use even things intended to destroy you.

The saying goes: "The battle is easy when you know your adversary." When we don't understand the nature and identity of what we are tackling, our efforts and actions may harm and destroy us. Today we live in a psychological and intellectual mode, speaking and acting in a way other people have converted into the standard. This has erased our personal ability to think, speak and act individually from other people. We watch television, but it doesn't watch us. Have you considered when you walk in the soccer stadium you are contributing to people expressing their gifts and making money? Have you discovered your gifts and doing what you should do to deploy yourself? People have succeeded in keeping our minds in a prison – and unproductively we listen and watch them, follow in their footsteps despite our uniqueness, diversities and individual purposes in life.

Remember the greatest evils in history were carried out by people who wrote the laws, not by those who broke them. Most of the world laws are only repressive; they relay the consequences we face for doing wrong, but there are no legal descriptions for remuneration for doing what is right. No-one legally secures a bonus for good driving, but you are punished for making mistakes. Essentially, the system does not reward you for being a good person – it punishes you for being a bad person, which is normal. However, good and bad has always been related, and something might be good for one person and bad for another person. It is a psychological fact that most people feel that they are right in whatever they do, just as slavery and colonialism were good and legal for those who institutionalised it. So your focus in life shouldn't be more about becoming bad or good, but it should rather be about accomplishing your mission. When you discover your true mission in this life, you will not have a reason to be a bad person, because we have all come from one source of love, kindness, righteousness and justice. We mostly stress about being good or bad because we are so concerned about what other people think and say when they look at us, and because we fear rejection. So we try our best to act only in the way that will be applauded by many people, which means that we begin to live to fit in to people's opinion without thinking about our individual purpose. This book will not teach you to be a bad person, but will revolutionise your perception of life and help you to manipulate the system to accomplish your mission. It will open your mind so you can see where you are supposed to go before you find somebody to take you in the wrong direction.

All people fall into these three categories: those who act, those who witness events and those who get surprised by events that occur. This book is my contribution to the numerous efforts engaged to uplift Africa and promote righteousness, justice and peace in the world. I hope that the readers who may find themselves in the third category, will find a necessity to move into the second and first category in order to take part in the architecture of our individual and common future. The worst thing to do is to do nothing, and that is what the system promotes through propaganda of fear and discouragement; however, beyond the fear, there is a hope.

1
Where it All Begins

"He who has no faith in others shall find no faith in them."
Chinese philosopher and writer, Lao Tzu (born 601BC)
"Those who seek should not stop seeking until they find. When they find, they will be disturbed. When they are disturbed, they will marvel and will reign over all and after they have reigned, they will rest."
The Book of Thomas

Every day offers us the unlimited power to observe, think and understand. When we observe a car moving, we understand someone dreamt of a car; developed that thought into an idea and, when well fertilised, became a project. Finally, the executed project evolved into creating a car. The same process applies to everything we see and do in the world: relationships, marriage, businesses or a house. Nothing has its roots in accidents, but is the fruit of creative minds and somebody's responsibility. What you want should be the fruit of your mind. It's an intellectual and spiritual dishonesty to acknowledge the existence of the universe, but deny it was somebody's thought and creation. I want to acknowledge God who brought creation into existence and to Him I render my worship by doing the work He assigned me. My mission is bringing back to life the mentally dead African man and woman. Regardless of the different names by which people address Him, He is the creator. Everything that exists in our world today first existed in His mind. He planned them and pragmatically brought them into a physical form. He has created everything and everyone for a purpose, one that always starts with the land, because without land there is no nation, no history, no identity or purpose.

Humans are the superior beings in creation with other creatures existing to serve us. Men rule the earth in serving the highest purpose of righteousness and justice. However, whenever fear replaces confidence in our minds, righteousness and justice become oppression to us and freedom becomes a trophy of wars. We shall leave the universe unpredictably, meaning everyone is treated equally by the universe. This should mean humans live with confidence and humanity without waging wars. When they lose confidence in the universal logic, they fear the unseen and unknown. Fearing tomorrow they perceive the only way to ensure the future is to control the resources. If those resources are owned by others, the perception is for that party to be conquered or eliminated through war to secure tomorrow. More broadly understood, the root of racial discrimination and injustice is the fear of the unknown – the fear of tomorrow that pushes us to wholly possess and leave others with nothing. We want to be strong, watching and maintaining others in their weakness. Thirsty for power, we like to extend our original power to have dominion over the earth, to its inhabitants like ourselves – but this was not the natural order God had ordained.

Consequently, few people today have more than enough with the masses existing to put meagre portions of bread on their tables – if at all. Sadly, those in power wage wars to retain it, while the masses endlessly seek out their liberty and power. No-one deserves to be labelled worthy for enslavement and anyone willingly accepting slavery lowers himself to a mere animal. The concepts of freedom and liberty should be everyone's target, especially if they are living under oppression and servitude, whether spiritual, psychological and physical.

Freedom

Everyone desires freedom, but no-one can provide it on behalf of another. In reality freedom does not exist. The concept as advertised has never existed, even when people overcome their oppressors. They merely get rid of a bad system to secure treatment from another considered as good, but they are still not totally and independently free. A son depends on his parents. When he wants to become independent (financially), he needs to find a job in order to provide for himself and therefore he becomes dependent on his job. Nobody is free.

In Christianity, those who denounce Satan to live with Christ are delivered and transferred from the kingdom of darkness to God's kingdom of light. Since every kingdom operates with laws and rules, membership demanding abiding by those laws – again, a person is not free. By definition, the word Islam means submission to the will of God and the followers of Islam are called Muslims, and are thus those who submit to the will of the one God. You cannot be free, whether or not you deny God. You will always hold on to some things for your existence; things like the sun, the air, the water, and, when that hold is withdrawn, you are subjected to its dominion.

Understand Everything Before Judging

We must learn from all things, systems and divinities to understand the laws and rules under which they operate. Thereafter we can choose to submit to those regulations compatible with our aspirations in life. People always belong to a system, but the creator of that system defines its laws while followers study and master them. It is when people want to establish a different logic the system turns on itself and conflicts arise.

Today people follow Jesus, Buddha, Muhammad or Moses. Others follow science, money or other forms by which they identify themselves and have found compatible with their life aspirations. Yet, the sad reality is many followers don't live according to the logic and laws outlined by the doctrine they profess to follow. Some don't even know what they are following and why. Essentially, there is only one force that brought everything into existence. It is the force supplying energy to the sun; power to the wind and everything about which man speculates – God the creator. He created the world to function as a balance between righteousness and unrighteousness so man can live in justice. When righteousness loses its balance to the benefit of unrighteousness, evil becomes fair because justice is reversed.

The Western Illusion

The western illusion of freedom as it's sold as democracy is a deception. It presents a freedom that denies the subjection of humans to any force superior to them. Africans have fought and embraced democracy, expecting total freedom where they live as they want; choosing their own leaders. Yet, the only right democracy provides today is the right to convert into something lower than their current status and the right for sex-confusion. If a person wants to become an animal or a male a woman and vice versa, democracy supports and assists that freedom. But it has not enabled millions of Africans to change their situation for the better. If someone tries to transform their life through emancipation, there is no democracy standing next to them in that struggle – and there is limited freedom to do so given the prejudice and paperwork. If democracy was really about freedom and emancipation, those who introduced the concept to Africa would have loved some of the leaders who helped their people become self-sustainable. The proof democracy is not designed for the freedom or good for Africans is apparent when we see its protagonists destroying any African leader involved in the development and self-determination of his people. What African democracy demands is not just the right to elect its own leaders who in most cases are preselected and showcased by the media, but the support that transforms ignorant people into self-determined nations. This is because the rise of weakened people cannot happen through strong institutions, but it can happen with strong people who build strong institutions compatible to their realities.

We have to understand the concept of freedom else spend our lives seeking something that does not exist. Consider the oxymoron – the people responsible for oppressing Africa are responsible for creating the system to restore our freedom and human rights. The outcome for being free without consequences and responsibilities can only translate into another nightmare. Liberty is the unique prerogative of God since He is the master of time and space, while humans are limited within their own resources and capabilities.

The Concept of Self-determination

Freedom equates to self-determination. This was the capacity God gave to man. Rather than being interpreted in line with the popular desires, it is a freedom born of the fruits of human productivity and creativity. Oppressed people do not lose their freedom but rather their self-determination and must be reminded of the nature in which they were created to evaluate the dimension destroyed in them. Accompanying slavery are numerous actions committed against individuals and nations that disable their capacity for self-determination. Restoring self-determination demands first engaging internally to identify the dimension that has stopped working. Africans must engage with each other before we can negotiate issues with our oppressors. Servitude never ends via negotiations, because only a slave can abolish slavery. If you are carrying a weight across your back, the only way to shift it is to stand straight up.

The fundamental concept of the self-determination is to live without fear. People's actions and reactions are emotionally based in line with happiness, sadness, anger, fear and shame. Oppressed people live in fear – and when people are hijacked by fear, the result is paranoia and anxiety. The survival mechanism becomes domination of those around them. Oppression through manipulation is the best way to dominate others, because man has an inherent pride. In conquering the opponent's pride, the relationship between oppressor and the oppressed is established. The man who loses his self-determination is the oppressor because, driven by fear, he aims to keep others in a position of weakness. It is this fear that witnesses the first world developed countries continuously investing in weapons of mass destruction. Their prejudice underpins their judgment of others. Only self-determination and the confidence to live peacefully regardless of diversities and the potential of other people, can replace fear. Neither the oppressor nor the oppressed are free - one is bound by fear and another limited by his incapacity to be self-determining due to the oppression.

2
The Self-determined People

"Always bear in mind your own resolution to succeed is more important than any other."
Former US president, Abraham Lincoln (1809-1865)

Anything that physically exists and any action, good or bad, have previously existed in the invisible world – in the minds of people. In other words, every activity or reality society currently faces is an expression of someone's mind. That is why if a society wants to eradicate crimes and injustice, it must invest more into people's minds than in building new prisons. By healing minds, society can be corrected and the most important element for people to grasp is self-determination.

Self-determination is the ability of men and women to function like God, essentially to self-create and become the result of their own free will and actions. Everyone is born through the same process and exposed to the same natural conditions, but the ability to design their own destiny determines the success of one person over another. It demands the knowledge, will, commitment and responsibility for their actions.

Self-determination is about self-knowledge, self-confidence and applied knowledge.

Self-knowledge

The knowledge of self is the source of energy that keeps people moving toward their destiny despite interferences with time, space and circumstances. The two elements building self-knowledge are history and culture. Every person, wherever they are or whatever they do, identify in the context of their history and culture. African American historian, professor and pioneer in the creation of pan-African and African studies, Dr. John Henrik Clarke (1915-1998) said, "History is not everything, but it is a starting point. History is a clock that people use to tell their political and cultural time of day. A compass people use to find themselves in the map of human geography. It tells them where and what they have been. History tells people where and what they are, but more importantly, what they must be. The relationship of history to people is the same as the relationship of a mother to a child."

People who remember their history and love their culture do not ask for position in a foreign system, but position themselves to accomplish a specific task to contribute to society. However, those who do not remember their history readily abandon their culture and purpose to embrace another one and can be easily destroyed. American Muslim minister and human rights activist Malcolm X (1925-1965) said people who stand for nothing fall for anything. People who believe in a future have to learn about their past to understand their present and plan their future.

Self-confidence

Self-determined people exude self-confidence and personally tackle tasks before counting on others for assistance. Anything one person has done can be improved by another including you. There is no-one who can feel your pain and you should be the one at the frontline of the fight for the solutions you want. However, you need confidence in your divine nature to make things happening. The self-confidence underpins your self-image, producing your character and behaviour to generate the results you want. Remember – you have everything you need and you are the one needed.

Applied Knowledge

Yet, before you come to applying knowledge, you must acquire it. In this information age ignorance is only a choice. Everyone has two responsibilities: learning and teaching. Specifically for Africans, we only emerge as self-determined once we have gained and applied the knowledge on which we previously depended on others to provide. There is a gap between knowing something and doing something. Knowledge is only power once applied. You may know the consequence of cigarette and alcohol use, but too few people apply the knowledge.

We cannot be uplifted as self-determining people without studying, exchanging and applying knowledge. The American author Neely Fuller Junior wrote, "All people, both white and non-white have persons among them who have great knowledge and understanding of many things, but non-white people do not consolidate and constructively utilise and efficiently exchange the things they have learned from time to time, they do not record and store what they learn, they allow what they learn to filter away, they do not pass on constructive information willingly, deliberately, constantly and efficiently to those who need it most, this is one of the reasons much of what non-white people once knew was lost and or forgotten." We must always try learn something about anything that exists in the universe, and we must also learn from our mistakes that have deviated us from our destiny and determine not to repeat them. Seek to know people and know how to deal with friends and enemies without turning your back on them.

3
Productivity

"If you think in terms of a year, plant seed; if in terms of 10 years, plant trees; if in terms of 100 years, teach the people."

Chinese philosopher, Confucius (551-479 BC)

It is essential to remember we live for a reason. What keeps you living is duty and when you have wholly accomplished that, you give justification to your existence. However, failing to do so deems your life less importance. Even an ant is better than a human who does not fulfil his purpose in efficiently using the gifts received. We have been given numerous tools in common to enable us to unite our individual gifts to realise our dreams. We have land, air, water and sunlight. From land you can grow food; with the air you can fly and create energy and with water. The only limits is your imagination. Most importantly remember to start with self-determination – and that demands investing in the mind. Only you can build or destroy your mind. Even Jesus knew this when he said: "As the man thinks so is he."

If someone calls you or even treats you as a negro, you are not destroyed by the treatment but how you allow your mind to interpret and mull over the thought that will be your undoing. The only way to prevent your mind from being programmed with wrong information is to feed yourself thoughts about what you are willing to do and become in life. Check what you see (the power of image) and what you hear (the power of words).

According to online site www.besteduchina.com, China produces 600000 engineers every year and according to the statistics from The World Christian Encyclopedia, Africa produces 12 million Christians every year. Twelve million pastors every year, yet Africans still struggle with witchcraft. It simply means while the number of preachers grow, so do the problems grow. Maybe we should be producing problem-solvers rather than just preachers. We should be more productive with our lives in exploring new ideas and methods to see where we can improve. In today's society, everything is on move and no-one can move forward by doing what was done 50 years ago. In the beginning God used three aspects: thought, word and action. He thought. He spoke and He created. A word is a spoken thought and a thought an unspoken word. When speaking to yourself, you are thinking out loud and when you are silent, you are thinking. God thought through His word and created through His actions. Becoming self-determined demands efficiently using the formula: head to hands, means, function from head to hands – essentially from thought to action and key to the process is thinking. Anyone becomes what they desire by applying the formula, but remains a slave to another by disregarding its application. Everyday activities are the products of either your own mind or another person's mind, yet what you do daily is what shapes your life and has the potential to change your reality for better or for worse. When you realise you are doing something not of your thinking, take time out to analyse your true value to the world and how you can improve it regardless of what others say and do. Anyone who sits down to use their mind has self-purpose, self-direction and self-vision. Anyone who works on the influence of somebody else's mind, journeys without direction, purpose or vision. In the long-term, his life has no purpose because he is accompanying and assisting someone else in their purpose, direction and vision. If you don't reflect on your life's direction and vision, you will spend your life serving other people's purpose. The musician plays music and controls the melody, but the dancer just dances to the music and follows the melody. The conqueror writes it and the conquered read the history.

We all have the same length of day and night; breathe the same air and use the same water under the same sun. Our differentiating factor is our ability to productively use our minds. Essentially everyone does something every day, but it's better to be productive than unproductive. Too many non-white people merely observe, watch, admire, buy, follow, trust and advertise other people's achievements. They are happy and willing to become members of other people's institutions rather than build and belong to something of their own.

Every person is meant to live from what he does with what he possesses. This corrupted system evolved from the success to divert minds away from their possessions and focus on what the system can present to them. Many African children today consider their land as worthless dust, yet European and Chinese investors repatriate this dust to produce cellphones – and then sell those cellphones back to Africa. They add value to our raw materials and earn the profits when that process is something we should be doing ourselves. Yet, in the eyes of young African children, they only see the valuable goods brought to their stores by the European or Chinese investors and perceive all good things come from abroad.

It underpins why the dreams of many young Africans are not anchored in Africa, but overseas and why some pray and fast as a request to God to bless them with the opportunity for obtaining an international visa. It also underpins why too few Africans take the time to develop Africa as they do not view the continent as holding their future. People always walk toward the point where they believe they can meet their future.

This raises the question about how many young Africans will participate in the reconstruction of Africa. There is a dramatic difference between wealth and money with the potential for anything to be called the latter only to find its value destroyed overnight and something else used in its place. However, wealth produces any form of money and the aberration of this system is those who do not have wealth have the power to print money. Those who own the wealthy African soil are the poorest and will willingly become like those who only print papers.

4
Expropriation of the Mind

"I cannot teach anybody anything. I can only make them think."
Greek philosopher Socrates (died 399BC)

This chapter tackles the thorny issue of land, a difficult and sensitive one particularly in the light of the current South African discussions around land expropriation without compensation. It analyses the scepticism among Africans based on their historical experience in Africa following the independence of former colonial empires. Across Africa, most countries were subject to the European invasion and systematic division of land then systematically exploited through an institutionalised servitude. These unjust treatments led to many Africans rising up to join the struggle against colonialism, itself a sophisticated form of slavery.

The liberation struggle and end to slavery triggered numerous African freedom fighters to expropriate the lands from Europeans or to ask for its repatriation. Since you cannot duel with the people who have destroyed you, Africans repossessed the lands the Europeans had previously taken away and controlled through force.

Across Africa only South Africa has not undergone a land expropriation and repatriation process following democracy and this underpins why the majority of South African citizens, together with some political parties, have called for expropriation without compensation. While this is not the subject of this book, knowing every person has a purpose in life realistically translates into everyone needing land on which and with which to accomplish that purpose. Land provides all our needs. Consequently, Africans want to regain control of their land as a physical reflection of being in charge. Land can be used, but not kept.

However, the apparent reality seems to be that those African countries who wanted to reclaim their land for their own purposes today record mass exoduses of their people to the countries from which their oppressors originated. Others settle in South Africa to escape the economic and political instability gripping their own countries, believing in a promising South African economy "handled by white people". Now, the calls for land expropriation without compensation has triggered fears among analysts that the country will suffer the same fate economically and politically as other African nations.

The importance of this discussion, whether or not I agree with the proposal for expropriation without compensation, is how it raises an often neglected aspect of the struggle for self-determination and success among many African intellectuals – the expropriation of the mind without compensation. The explanation of this concept might profoundly impact on the way in which you consider your life and use the tools you have been given. Since the intention of this book is to address different people across their beliefs, the discussions into which I engage should approach every subject from diverse aspects – spiritually, scientifically, psychologically and physically depending on the message. People are more than physical; they embody a spirit, soul and body.

The Torah, Bible and Quran all explain men and women were created from the earth. Men and women are parts of the earth, because they were taken from earth. The earth yields a wealth of value including gold, diamonds and minerals required to produce precious metals. By extrapolation, every man and woman walking the earth, whether they sleep in palace or under the bridge, holds gold, diamonds, platinum and silver within their being. Hence, before searching underground, dig within yourself to find your precious materials. The same things triggering wars for their worth in the earth are found in you and me. We were taken from earth and have traces of the earth's precious elements in us. Therefore, it is virtually impossible for you to produce and manage goods coming out of the earth if you haven't discovered and know how to use your own value. Even if you hold all the world's gold or diamonds in your hands, you can do nothing with them beyond selling them to a willing a buyer. Discovering your inner worth helps you understand the capabilities in your hands and the role you play among other people. You will know what you can do with the wind, water, sun, herbs, land and minerals.

Discovering your precious metals is the same process geologists use to uncover the earth's treasures. They repeatedly and objectively explore the land through prospecting. Do the same introspectively – you are the geologist of your life. Too many people are stuck in life because they want to be discovered by others, but this is not the way it works. Can you imagine, despite Christ accomplishing numerous beautiful things for His people, the community turned on Him and claimed He was demon-possessed, healing people by the power of Beelzebub, the prince of demons? How then do you think people can discover your true self merely because you pray it will happen? If other people discover in you the gold you didn't discover, they will use it for their gain without you even knowing or benefiting from it.

Sometimes the only gold or diamonds in your life are what the world has classified as a handicap. If you wait on the world to discover you, it will label you as handicapped, but if you search out your true self, you have the opportunity to turn your handicap into handi-capable. Your discovery may be spiritual, psychological and/or physical, but the most important aspect is for it to be more explored within the domain of your mind.

Scientifically talking, psychologists have defined the mind as equal to the land and a thought equal to planted seeds. When you can't extract precious materials from the earth, you can still use the land for other purposes. You can plant and fertilise seeds and it will produce more than what you planted. The mind functions in the same way. If you ponder on its operation, think about what people do with the land and, most importantly, question why they fight over it? Then you will understand the reason underpinning racism. Once you plant and study thoughts, you fertilise those thoughts into ideas that shift into projects and visions to be pursued and achieved. Yet, the rider to that reality is negative, harmful thoughts like racism can also fertilise and grow.

Everything in this world, whether natural or artificial, is the fruit of the mind. Anything that has happened to you was the fruit of the mind. Anything you do from now on in your life still is the fruit of the mind, but this time it will be the fruit of your own mind. I don't believe you, in all good spirit, can plant destructive seeds in your mind unless driven by aggressors. This is the case for many Africans and thus the reason we are discussing the expropriation of the mind without compensation.

God has sent everyone with a purpose, no matter our titles. Into that realm we need to understand these titles must not confuse you, especially when you don't have one. God has sent us all here for a purpose and assignment – and no matter what the purpose is, it will always start with the land. Remember, the most important land is your mind then the earth. We have been made to live from the land; have a means to eat from the land; have clothes to wear because of the land; build houses from and on the land; work the land to die first from the land (mind) and be physically buried in the land. That's why the first blessings God declared to man were related to the land (Gen 1:28), the natural dominion and power to rule given to man was over the land and not other people. This means you were made to dominate firstly your mind, but not to dominate or to be dominated by others. There is nothing you can become or obtain that does not come from the land. The greatness and honour you seek do not come from prophesy or long prayers, but is related to land use – and that is first in your mind and secondly from the earth.

Our task is to learn about and know how to use the land, because when you don't take care of and cultivate your territory, it will grow a myriad of herbs and bushes that finally evolves into a forest filled with often dangerous reptiles, insects and animals. It changes names to become a jungle, a place where there is no civilisation, peace and definitely no humanity. Hence, it's your responsibility to control what grows in your land by sowing the type of seeds that can produce the results you want to reap. Remember when I'm talking about the land, it's first your mind followed by your territory. When you don't control and plant in your mind thoughts corresponding to your aspiration, it will grow thoughts likely to turn your mind against you and society.

If you are unable to discover your precious material, at least know how to plant seeds and reap your fruits. Otherwise you will find it difficult to figure out what you can do with your physical land and anything that may come from it.

5
Destroying with Negligence

"If you don't know how to live, why wonder about death?"
Chinese philosopher, Confucius (551-479 BC)

Many people die without discovering and unrevealing their gifts and talents, leaving their minds unexplored. It's not just an external enemy who wants to destroy them, but that they have destroyed themselves by neglecting their talents. You can destroy a garden simply by not watering it; you can destroy a relationship simply by not giving the attention it needs. Similarly, we can destroy our potentials by neglecting them. The principle is simple – anything you have and don't use, doesn't belong to you and anything in you not used, dies. Any gift or talent you possess, but don't want to use will stop functioning. Even your brain left devoid of exercise by not solving problems, will die. If you immobilise your leg in one position for a long time, it will cease to function and you will not be able to use it again.

As Africans, we have neglected our potentials, human and assets, because we craved the imported ones. We complain daily for Europeans looting African resources, but equally we are not willing to think creatively about how we can use the natural resources we have. We scramble for European, American and Chinese goods and reassurances. The reality is Africa does not belong to Africans, because we don't use it beyond in burial. The Bible states more will be given to the one who has, but the one who has nothing, even what he has, will be taken and given to the one who have. If you have nothing, what else can and will be taken from you? Will your life and dignity be stripped from you and be put to the disposal of someone else who has ensured his life is more productive? That is why we have people who spend their lives being used – they didn't find out what to do with their own lives. Africa did not die because of European invasion and the enslavement of

Africans. Wars, enslavements and invasions have happened throughout history to every people and most of them recovered, but no people in recorded history have found themselves in conditions of alienation and psychosis as many black people exist today. It is a condition I call mental death. Africa died when Africans accepted foreign make-ups and began to neglect their lands psychologically and physically and intended to use ideas and dreams painted by Europeans. That was the beginning of our mental death. We wanted to use the concepts and minds of people we thought were friends, but later revealed themselves as our oppressors. When people use their oppressors' minds, they oppress themselves.

Humanity emphasises hard work as the way to success, but does not explain the difference between working too much and working hard. A hard worker follows the formula head to hands. He engages the mind first, then the word and action. It's hard, but the good news is it doesn't last beyond completing the job. Hard work solves societal issues as much as it solves personal ones. However, working too much reverses the process and happens when people ignore their mental faculties to focus on their hands. When you only want to engage your hands, you are only preparing yourself for employment not deployment. Working with the hands should be the final stage of materialisation for something created originally in the mind. Everyone has the capacity to bring something new into his field of activity and speciality, but the average person will focus on what he can do with his hands, because exercising the brain to invent something is difficult. Working too much gets you nowhere in this life; it only means you are used as the bridge for other people to reach financial freedom while you remain static. Don't neglect yourself, because you are a major contribution to the growth of humankind and every time you don't do what you are meant to do, you are neglecting your potential. By doing this, you automatically become a major contribution to the instability of society, as many people will be suffering from your negligence. Don't neglect your children, do the best you can to invest in them because investment in any person especially with money, is not a loss; that's why it's called human capital. The World Bank has created what is called the human capital index; according to Jean-Christophe Carret, the World Bank director in central Africa, their researches show that every 1US dollar invested in nutrition for a person, produces 11US dollars benefit. Sometimes in life becoming a source of joy to many people can be a measurement for success. If you give 1US dollar to a person who has 10 000US dollars, it's just an ordinary act, but if you give the same 1US dollar to a person who lives in misery and poverty, it's firstly an extraordinary blessing for the person and secondly, it's an investment which will produce a benefit to society. It will cost you only 10US dollars per week to become a source of joy for 10 people and to make a major contribution to society, so please don't neglect yourself, as it doesn't really need millions, but it starts just with you.

6
Africa Needs a Man Next to a Woman

"In the end we will remember not the words of our enemies, but the silence of our friends."

American Baptist minister and activist, Martin Luther King Jr (1929-1968)

Every achievement in the world is a fruit of the mind. Humans are capable of great things if they function in the way they are intended. The three items involved in creating anything in life are the mind (thoughts), mouth (words) and hands (actions) with the mind used efficiently being the most powerful. This is because before your hands start working, the mind must have created the intended actions. If you want to realise how powerful your mind is, think about the strength and speed of a missile – and then remember it was the result of the mind's creation. Equally important is the theory of recessive and dominant that states nothing dominant can emerge from a recessive thing, but only recessive can emerge from the dominant. Essentially, your mind is more powerful than anything it creates and only requires a thought and a word to shift into action. Thoughts cannot stand without words since words are the expressions of thoughts and actions the demonstration of thoughts plus words. Yet, no matter how powerful the mind can be, it can also be destroyed by a simple word. Words are powerful, as in most cases our emotions and thoughts are created by what we hear. If you can analyse the origin of the suffering black people have gone through, you will find it in words. This is because people who know themselves cannot be turned into something else by brutality, but only by a lie told in words. In 1831 a German philosopher, Friedrich Hegel, who had never visited Africa said: "Africa is a country where men are like children, a land away from the light of its own historical consciousness, ruled by the dark colour of night, Africa does not belong to the world's history."

Richard Francis Burton, a British explorer who visited Africa said: "The study of blacks is the study of the human mind at its most rudimentary stage, people which resemble more to a degeneration of a civilized man. Their naturalness is unfit for education or culture they seem to belong to one of those infantile species which cannot accede to the condition of man". Some years back in the American constitution, black people were qualified as 3/5 of a free man. These words among many others created concepts, beliefs and perceptions in the minds of black people which conditioned them to live below their abilities without self-confidence and therefore anything Europeans bring, will be regarded as civilization. Many black people still believe this today without questioning. That has been and still is the impact of words.

The same word that destroys a mind can also restore it if used differently. Creation always needs a combination of thoughts and words with thought as the seed and word the fertiliser bringing it to life. Thought represents man and word woman with the intercourse of the two creating life. A man can become successful, but he cannot become great without a woman next to him, just as thought cannot be known without word. They compete equally in the creation process as the sun and moon. The sun runs the day and the moon the night. If the sun had to rule alone, daytime would be endless and innovation and transformation impossible as it is during the night that life regenerates and most of the greatest inspirations come into being. Daytime is the realisation and accomplishment of what was born and decided at night.

We must acknowledge the place and role women play in society and in our lives. Even in this struggle for the liberation of Africa, we need a large involvement from African women as their strong emotional energy is the key to success. Can you imagine being unfaithful to your woman when she is away but still willing to sacrifice herself financially to bail you out of trouble? This scenario is not the same in reverse simply because women are too emotional and hold their power in emotions. If they harness that emotional energy in this liberation struggle, they will neither compromise nor betray. Whenever women have entered the struggle, they have changed the social reality – American activist Rosa Parks remembered for her role in the Montgomery bus boycott; South African activist Winnie Mandela also known for her role internationally in keeping former president Nelson Mandela's story in the headlines while the apartheid government had hidden him away in jail; Yaa Asantewaa, the queen mother of the Ejisu in the Ashanti Empire now modern-day Ghana who led her people in War of the Golden Stool against the British colonialists in 1900 and Nzinga Mbande, the 17th century queen who demonstrated an aptitude for defusing political crises. Recognising women, respecting them and taking care of them in society is not a favour; it's their right.

7
Taking Charge

"You can't build a reputation on what you are going to do."
American entrepreneur, Henry Ford (1863-1947)

The pathway to freedom I call self-determination starts with us accepting our responsibilities and taking charge of our lives. Chinese philosopher, Confucius, is credited with the statement: "When we meet people of a contrary character, we should turn inwards and examine ourselves." This means only we can be in charge of our lives and the atmosphere around us. The only time you can determine the result of something is when you are in charge. Taking charge happens in three phases – realising your potential; taking care of that potential and using your potential.

Realisation

For realisation to happen, you must take a self-inventory, not of your possession, but primarily your spiritual and moral identity and then your physical or materialistic identity. This process demands self-questioning and self-answering. Everything achieved in this universe happens via questions and answers. Similarly, you must question your reasons for existence and the value you can add to humanity. In conducting personal checks on the inputs, you can bring to society through ordinary conversations and meetings, you realise your potential and role in society. It's in this moment you relocate yourself in the map of human geography. You uncover an understanding of your spiritual, mental and physical potential and can confidentially rise to do what God has demanded of you.

Taking Care of Your Potential

After you have realised your potential, you may discover yourself in a position where you are unable to use them given your current realities. In this situation too many people abandon their ways, returning to what they had done previously to survive despite an unwillingness to do so. Most people settled in the survival mode do not pursue personal ideals, but produce for other people's benefit. You must take care of your gift and potential. Read books and research it; keep it alive or improve it. Dedicate practice time and offer free services so others can ameliorate what you have. Never give up or neglect your potential, because it's the reason for which God brought you in this universe. Remember, if you don't live for your purpose, you live without justification.

Use Your Potential

When you have discovered your potential kept alive the flame, the third step is using it at every opportunity, even creating your own chances. Begin small but slowly and you will reach the right point. However, the system is not well-set to receive newcomers; it will resist you, but you must impose yourself over the system. You must lose yourself and release your passion for something for which you have been waiting. If everybody has done it well, you must exceed their achievements for there is no reason to exist in only doing well something already done well.

You don't wait unprepared for the opportunity experience or explore. Rather you are well-prepared for opportunities to prevent missing them. Too often we wait for the *big bang* in our lives to realise the time has come to move towards something important. Yet, the reality is every day presents a myriad of small important things on which we can act, forgetting the small pieces add up to a large difference.

The power and gifts that can make our lives flourish do not come from outside, but are sleeping within us. It is a built-in capacity and we must use those talents now for worthwhile reasons.

8
Take What Belongs to Caesar and Make it Yours

"How can you tell people to not break the policies if the first law of nature is self-preservation?"

Louis Farrakhan (born 1933)

If you think someone else holds the power to free you from your struggles, you make that person your ruler. If you believe your solution lies with someone else, you are making yourself a prisoner to another. Too many people claim money makes the world go round, but in reality, if you hide $1 million dollars, only you know how to find it. When you return five years later, that $1 million will be where you left it. It did nothing to the world. It didn't function and obviously didn't produce or buy anything. However, when it re-enters your hands, it obtains the power to make the world go around – you can buy things and employ people. Money has power and value when it touches your hands. Essentially, you make the world go round and not pieces of paper inscribed with words and a person's image. Nothing in the world has power until you give it that power. Institutions only have the power we have given to them. For European countries to be able to manipulate and dominate African people, they must first strip Africans of their power of self-determination and the power to be in charge. They just don't strip them of power, but appropriate themselves with that power. European countries have looted African resources to flourish, while millions of Africans live in abject poverty and struggle against various forms of difficulties while living on some of the richest earth in the world.

The power oppressors have is the power Africans have given to them, willingly or unwillingly. The power the Devil uses to oppress people is the same power men gave to him, according to the Torah, Bible and Quran. In Africa's case we are dealing with a dangerous and destructive institution called white supremacy, an ideology mistreating people based on their skin colour. It has no other power to destroy except the power we give it.

White supremacy has positioned itself in charge of everything in the same way Caesar was in charge. Receiving the people's power to rule, Caesar had certain requirements to meet the people's aspirations and if they weren't repaid, they had indicated in unequivocal terms they would take all from Caesar and make it their own. Genevan philosopher, writer and composer Jean-Jacques Rousseau said: "When the poor have nothing to eat, they have only rich men as food."

When legal experts were asked to find Jesus guilty, He asked for a silver coin and asked the assembled crowd what the image and inscriptions were. They replied the image and inscriptions belonged to Caesar to which Christ replied: "Give to Caesar what belongs to Caesar and give to God what belongs to God." (Matthew 22:21).

This scripture, along with numerous others, has been given the wrong interpretation and is the reason why we have given up our rights and responsibilities in society. We ask for favours when we have the right to change things. The only thing belonging to Caesar is his coin. Return the coin and he no longer has power over you. The simple question is: "Why are our lives messed up even though we are doing everything the system asks us to do?"

The answer is we are mostly doing things wrong, because we respond without knowledge, wisdom or perception. We are enacting Caesar's mind to his benefit. We have given him our belongings, even those that belong to God – and the most important thing we gave away was our minds. We have given Caesar our humanity for which he gave us a silver coin decorated with his image and inscriptions. The outcome is we have no justice, peace, jobs, economy, healthcare, manhood, womanhood or power. We only have a worthless silver coin reflecting Caesar's image. Everything else he invented only facilitates his dominion over us. Whether we are discussing democracy, the United Nations, national and international laws, banks and banking systems, education or black economic empowerment, there are problems. There are educational programmes offered that provide qualifications without competence; we are presented with rules made by people who have power and who do not want to see Africans achieving better than they have done. Policies are regulated that effectively prevent people from achieving their potential. The educational system and social structures impose a single way of thinking, but consistently shift the goal posts, meaning our mental faculties are manipulated at will. We blindly follow because we are not allowed to – nor been taught how to – think outside the box. Caesar has robbed millions of young Africans of their creative minds, forcing them to view their lands as valueless and prompting a willingness and desperation to swim the Mediterranean Sea to seek a better life.

Africa's natural potential should reflect our ability to possess powers the world typically does not want to see in black hands. Caesar agreed to give black Africans independence after years of servitude and oppression, because he knew they would do nothing with it. He had retained our minds. As a youth, I visited my grandparents in their village where they farmed chickens and it was my duty to care for the fowls. I had to release them from their coups each morning and return them in the evening. Occasionally we purchased new chickens unfamiliar with their coup and the house, so I couldn't release them immediately as they would never return. Consequently, I tied them to the coup hatch and had-fed them for four days before releasing them. The irony is despite those chickens having been held captive for four days, they never ran away, but returned each evening to the place where they had been held.

This is the condition in which many black people find themselves today. We have been psychologically conditioned to be owned and used as private property by people who have destroyed our ability for self-management. The true struggle should focus on this aspect rather than on reclaiming the materials we don't know how to use. We have embarked on a wrong process for the right reason, namely liberating

Africa, but have settled for assets. We march to demand jobs, healthcare, economy and free education, but do less for the liberation of our humanity, dignity and distinctive identity as African people. As Senegalese historian, anthropologist, physicist and politician, Cheikh Anta Diop said: "Your enemy kills you first spiritually, morally, before he kills you physically." The European invaders did not only take our lands, but also our central humanity, personalities and dignities – essentially the totality of our minds, were taken hostage. They stripped away and slaughtered our personal confidence and capacity to create the life we want.

Now is the time to take back what was stolen; that which we gave willingly to Caesar. Africans are still being stripped of the key elements that have made the world what it is today. The system under which we operate is designed to squash our rise, despite our longing to take back from Caesar what we gave him. We must realise we don't benefit from Caesar and it is thus necessary to take back our belongings. This is not a physical or violent looting, but a psychological one where we reclaim ownership of the minds we have lost.

In secondary school a classmate stole his friend's phone. His crime was discovered; the police were called and the boy was taken into custody and locked up. Around 7pm that night the officer-in-charge gave the boy money and instructed him to go to the shop and buy him a cigarette. The boy walked a long distance, but couldn't see the shop. He returned to the officer and said he couldn't find the shop, but the officer sent him back out with the instruction to check again. The boy retraced his steps, but returned with the same explanation. This time the officer told him he had been given the chance to walk free but had not seized it and would therefore spend the night in custody.

There are numerous moral lessons to be drawn from the story, but my key message is if we don't do something today for our self-determination when we have the opportunity to do so, we are returning future generations to the cruellest servitude imaginable. We have the chance to grasp control of the system in a way that prevents others from being harmed. It is possible to accomplish our dreams, but the sad reality is those in power will never abandon their position. Regaining power will not happen via negotiation and only you can decide right path for you. Only a slave can abolish slavery. Today Caesar hugs your back and needs to be shrugged free from his hold over you. Whatever happens in the world deals with Caesar as you tackle white supremacy. Return Caesar's silver coin and replace his currency with something else to eliminate his dominion and power over you. Stop buying from Caesar to make your own things and you will not have to beg for jobs or emancipation.

Urban legend suggests when a Chinese person purchases an iPhone, it is not to take selfies, but for him to dismantle it so tomorrow he can produce his own replica. I saw a Facebook post where a preacher was evangelising to a Chinese man. He asked the man if he knew Jesus to which the man replied: "Bring me a sample and I will make you a cheaper one."

This is the mentality we have to adopt to take down Caesar. We need personal re-education. What is your vision in the company for which you are working? Are your eyes open to every activity and opportunity, learning from what has assisted others to succeed and applying the same principles? Applied knowledge is power. Learn and apply to produce personal power since it is power we need as Africans. The biggest scam perpetrated against Africans has been to make us believe our governments will do everything for us, disarming us from thinking and actively participating in the life of our continent and impacting on our individual lives. It is time to punish the Caesar in governments by applying this principle – whatever the government is not doing for us, we must do ourselves.

9
What is Justice?

"I'm for truth, no matter who tells it. I'm for justice, no matter who it is for or against. I'm a human being, first and foremost, and as such I'm for whoever and whatever benefits humanity as a whole."

American Muslim minister, Malcolm X (1925-1965)

As African intellectuals we are concerned about and working towards finding solutions to our problems. The first solution to any problem is acknowledging a problem exists and the fundamental problem facing non-white people is white supremacy. White supremacy is about mistreating others based on their skin colour. It's a lack of justice in society and therefore our efforts must be directed not to creating a black (or any other type of) supremacy, but to restoring justice. Apart from popular definitions of "justice", I propose a conceptual definition based on the nature in which everything functions. When the power of righteousness equals the power of unrighteousness, the result is justice. God structured the universe on the balance of justice. There are always two forces of the same, but opposing, magnitude required to maintain equilibrium. For a person to stand in equilibrium, he/she needs a left and a right leg in equal balance. To see clearly, he/she needs a left and a right eye with the same magnitude. This is the principle God applied to establish the standard of justice in life.

God established the two forces – negative and positive. Righteousness and unrighteousness are the forces represented by the choices good and bad in people's minds. According to the history of creation as recited in Genesis, God gave to man what He wanted, but He deliberately left the prerogative of choice with man. He placed man in the Garden of Eden and presented him with the choice of life represented by righteousness and the choice of death represented by unrighteousness. However, God's desire was for justice to prevail. Justice comes into existence when these two opposite forces are equal. Since the forces are supposed to be in balance, for one to increase means the other decreases.

In today's society too many people's mindsets are not in balance. Righteousness has decreased in favour of unrighteousness as the followers of the latter have risen. Evil has become the *laissez-faire* across every level of life and the result of this unbalanced system has deemed some people inferior in the eyes of others to enable them to justify oppression. The righteousness has lost its balance and we live in a world where people practicing injustice have more power over those practicing justice. The power of those practicing injustice came at the expense of those practicing justice. We constantly supply their power through the non-productive activities in which we engage daily. Therefore, it's our duty to stand firm and take back our power to restore righteousness. If our society is destabilised by the wickedness of people we know, the same society is destroyed by the silence and inaction of those standing on the side of righteousness – and that happens to be you and me.

How did we lose our power? We lost it when we bought what they sold; they sang and we danced. They sold us various forms of injustices through systems, institutions, education and food across the nine areas of activities identified by author and researcher, Dr Neely Fuller Jnr., namely: education, religion, economy, law, entertainment, sex, politics, labour and war. Notably, there is minimal to no one area among these nine where the righteous – and specifically Africans – have control. We are consistently dictated, directed, controlled and dominated by the unrighteous, becoming mere buyers even if it is poison. Other than perhaps medicine and vaccines, to my belief, there is very little Europeans have brought to Africa that was meant for our good, but rather introduced to facilitate their dominion over non-white people. They did nothing for the sake of justice. White supremacy has no hold without black people – and the reality is black people are indirectly supporting and maintaining the system. We have always wanted others to do for us what we should be doing ourselves. When the day arrives where Africa manufactures and sells her own products that we currently import, the system will eradicate foreign sellers, placing those companies into liquidation.

If we consider the concept of justice as explained by Fuller, justice is guarantying that no one is mistreated and those most in demand of help, receive the most constructive help they need. However, you are the first person who can guarantee you are not mistreated by playing your part for the sake of justice and righteousness. If you don't care about it, you might become the next victim of injustice.

10
Identity

"One of the greatest diseases is to be nobody to anybody."
Roman Catholic nun and missionary, Mother Teresa (1910-1997)

I entered the bank carrying my money in my pockets. I wanted to open an account to deposit my cash, but was asked for my identity document (ID). I tried purchasing a car with my cash, but they still wanted me to provide ID. In today's society, there are few things you can buy or sell without an ID, a book or smartcard containing your personal information. Its value is crucial as not having one makes it virtually impossible to acquire certain things even if you have the money. This condition is not limited to the ID book or smartcard, but extends to almost every area of our lives. Essentially, you cannot afford to live without the knowledge of who you are, as it allows others to make of you what they think you should be. In religious circumstances, many people pray to God for things they already possess without realising it simply because they don't know their own identify. As a black person you may over-use the word "black" because it describes your skin colour and physical appearance, but it doesn't tell you who you are. The knowledge of your identity reveals your purpose for existence, so when you discover who you are, you will in the same way discover who you are not.

A popular religious claim is that God wants to fill His kingdom with people; therefore, religions prepare their followers for the coming of paradise. Logic tells me if this was God's only concern, He would transfer babies directly from their mothers' wombs into His kingdom before they came to test sin on earth. In allowing us to come on earth to learn and grow, He demonstrates His desire for us to identify our individual purpose and reason for embracing this world.

Our lives only have meaning when we discover those reasons, but too few understand why we exist as we lack the knowledge of our identity.

We live aimlessly, wandering in the crowd or as easily joining another crowd when the mood determines. We adopt any advertised style; strive to fit into classes and if the latest style demands walking naked down the streets, we blindly follow suit.

Whenever someone ignores their identity, those around them thrust on them one that suits their needs. Whenever someone denies their identity, they become ignorant of their reality and live in another one. Even worse is believing they need to photocopy somebody else's life, because they merely become a psychological prisoner of the person imitated.

As humans, we have three identities – spiritual, psychological and physical.

Spiritual Identity

Spiritual identity is how we appeared in God's mind before we came into existence. We are born without knowledge, culture, language or religion, but with a purpose defined by our identity.

Psychological Identity

Psychological identity is our conceptions and belief system; it determines how we react differently from each other under the same situation. It's underpinned by our history, culture and knowledge and is what we see when we close our eyes.

Physical Identity

Physical identity is how the world sees us; our physical appearance. More importantly, it's how we express our belief in the society and, if you want to know who somebody is, check what he does.

To succeed in life the three identities must be connected in line with concepts and expressions. Many people fail because they are one thing spiritually, another psychologically and a third physically. You have to know who you are spiritually; build your belief system based on your uniqueness and act accordingly for success to prevail. People sometimes adhere to a religious doctrine as a means to seek protection from the devil. In their imagination the devil is a scary image, something not necessarily true in reality because the devil lives in the same religions without being recognised. He is proficient at disguising his identity. Job 2:1 says: "When the sons of God presented themselves before God, the devil was also there, but they didn't see him because he looked just like them."

Your problem is not what you don't see, but the correct identification of what you have seen and to accomplish that correctly, you must first identify yourself. When you look in the mirror, who do you see? To know yourself is to know God, because we are one with God. He is the creator who made us in His image.

People who lack self-knowledge cannot easily discover and accept their talents and skills, unless other people accept them. They cannot see good in themselves, their skin colour, names, cultures and traditions. This is especially relevant for Africans since our image has been attributed to the devil's identity, while God, Jesus and angels were portrayed as white. That's one reason why a black person considers it easy to burn another black person whose only crime is to be a foreigner. Yet, if someone discovers his identity and learns to value life, it is impossible for that person to kill another as he sees himself in the potential victim.

A man who knows himself does not need another leader; only his self-knowledge can lead him. We hold on to things or people to fill an emptiness created by an ignorance of our identity. Even in the absence of self-knowledge, our mind unconsciously holds on to something to fill the gap self-knowledge should hold. In some cases, people use religion as their point of identification, but what difference really exists between two Christians or two Muslims in terms of the individual identity of each person if all of them hold one religion to be their identity? Equally, what is the identity of a man and a woman in terms of creation given that organised religion came into being long after God created us in His image? We existed long before Judaism, Christianity and Islam evolved as organised religious practices. In Matthew 7:24 Jesus says: "Whoever hears my words and puts them into practice is like a wise man who builds his house (meaning his culture or identity) on the rock."

We don't have to put aside our African names, languages and cultures to please God, because He created people and cultures. Rather, He wants us to build our cultures on the foundation of His word. Remember, there are mathematical principles like fractal that have assisted in revolutionising technology and they were discovered through African cultures. Learn about yourself; be yourself; love who you are and find your place in the map of human geography.

You Are Not the Product of an Accident

Car manufacturers do not install equipment and accessories that will not boost the product's value. Doing so is a waste of money as parts require time and investment for their production. The same principle holds for humanity in its diversity. Your colour, body shape and character differences have been included for a reason. Geneses 1:3 states God created everything with His word by saying: "Let it be," and it was – the sun, moon, stars, water and wind were all made possible via a simple word from God. However, in creating man and woman, God summonsed the counsel of His highest divinity and said: "Let us make a man."

He called this meeting to discuss creating man, deciding on all the details of how men and women should be made including skin colour, body shape, thick lips and big noses. No part of you exists by chance. What the world defines as ugliness is according to people's standards and not God's purpose. If, by a simple word, God created the beautiful sun and stars, why would He make you into something ugly? If you believe you are merely the product of sexual intercourse between your parents, remember that out of millions of sperm only one made it to the egg to fertilise it and create you. You are more wonderfully and beautifully made than the sun or moon – nothing can be magnificent in God's eyes than you. He didn't just allow you to become a man or woman, but took time to shape you. Now you need to learn the reason for your every molecule and use them. Discover the previously concealed doors through your smile or beautiful voice. Use your beauty constructively to restore righteousness and justice in the world.

Your entire being, whether deemed ugly or beautiful in the world, is meant to serve you in accomplishing your destiny, specifically to serve humanity. However, you matter the most with God deeming it the order of the world for you to be greater than the other creatures; for them to serve you and you to serve God and Him alone.

Both the Bible and Torah relate how Satan rebelled against God in heaven and was thrown out to logically become the enemy of God and all His angels. In reality, Satan does not fight the angels or God directly; he fights man and his efforts are directed to dominating and destroying humanity. Satan saw in man God's attributes and glory. He found God's throne that he had initially wanted to possess in heaven. He recognised men and women are the carriers of God's glory and attributes. Our lives glorify God; the angels sing to glorify God, but we were also not created to merely sing and dance to His glory because we are already His glory. That's why it's shameful in God's eyes for a man or woman to bow down and worship anything other than God, as it diminishes God's glory in what He created.

The Bible says originally God's spirit moved on the water; had His throne based on water, but because the water was fluid, the spirit was moving on water. What then is the spirit of God? It is the power that brings the invisible into existence in our visible world. It has the power to create and water is the source of life. Nothing, regardless of how large or small, can live without water. The human brain is 75% water meaning your head is the throne of God. If we want to profoundly change our society, we must return God to the throne. Too many people speak about God, but they have replaced Him on throne with something else. Satan is on the throne and consequently, fear, greed, filth and all kinds of evil occupy the throne of many people.

Psalms 89:14 states righteousness and justice are the foundations of God's throne. This means putting God on the throne requires changing our mindset to embrace righteousness and justice. Our daily plans and activities must make us the defenders and promoters of justice and righteousness. Since today's world functions on principles based in injustice and unrighteousness, the church cannot work according to the world's agenda, but be driven by the desire to restore justice and righteousness. This is the real revolution to which we are being called, but too few churches claiming to stand for Christ's principles are willing to enter this revolutionary fight. They are avoiding tackling the real issue, specifically the system in which we are currently living. Revolution is not easy. It is not a big business, but a sacrifice. Throughout history anyone challenging the status quo with revolutionary concepts that fundamentally change the condition of oppressed people, has been swiftly targeted by those unwilling to see their privilege destroyed. Yet, today's churches are tasked with ensuring justice and righteousness is restored in the world. They are not meant to be obeying and pandering to a system preserving the status quo and contributing to the continued suffering of the oppressed. Christ said: "Whoever wants to save his life will lose it, but the one who loses his life for my sake will save it."

In concluding this discussion about identity, remember man was created in the Creator's profile with a productive power and the ability to bring into existence anything they can imagine. Key to that privilege is bringing back into our world justice and righteousness. Too few religious teachings push people into taking charge, rather helping people to suffer peacefully. When challenged about those people's desire to shrug off that cloak of poverty to live a wealthy life, the response too often condemns wealth as belonging to the devil and dissuades thoughts of self-improvement.

Luke 4:5 is cited as back-up whereby the devil lifted up Jesus on the mountain and showed Him all the kingdoms of earth and their glories. Then he instructed Christ to "bow down and worship me and I will give you all these". However, the argument falls short when considered with the following passage where the devil says: "I will give you all these because they have been given to me". The question is who had given those things to the devil? The answer is man because when God made man, He gave him the earth and the power to rule over it. Hence, in putting the devil on the throne, man automatically submitted to him and gave away his properties. But the good news for those who claim to believe in Jesus, is that they should be happy, because Jesus is called the restorer. When something is restored, it's put back exactly to its initial position. This means those who believe in Christ, have been restored into their initial ability with everything that the devil stole from them. If people still believe that the wealth and power belong to devil, they question their faith and their books. Africans generally, and Christians particularly, are unwilling to dominate any part of the whole planet. They focus rather on survival and tell their followers to suffer peacefully because Jesus will return to end our suffering. Yet, who is Jesus? That is the subject of the next chapter.

11
Who is Jesus?

"You shall know the truth and the truth will set you free."
Jesus Christ (John 8:32)

Today the name Jesus raises some controversies among many Africans, since Christianity was used in the transatlantic slave trade. This chapter attempts to present my understanding of who the true Jesus is compared to the European form typically presented and especially in Africa. Most Africans who hold Jesus responsible for what happened across Africa – the slave trade, colonisation and oppression – have not really had the chance to know Him. They probably have not even read the Torah, Bible or Quran and in not having read any of those religious texts, they cannot assume one or any of those religions are wrong, since they have no knowledge of the subject. Only in reading and studying those texts can anyone attempt to separate the good from the bad.

I have read the three texts and these views are based on the revolutionised African concept of Christ. My studying revealed the people who pretended to bring the message of Jesus to Africa neither intended nor wanted to do His word. Rather they put into action Christ's warning: "Many will come in my name, not to serve me but to accomplish their own purposes".

The first slave ship that ripped Africans from their homeland on the shores of West Africa and transported them across the Atlantic Ocean to a new world of hostility in the West Indies was named *Jesus of Lübeck*.

She was a carrack built in the early 16th century and acquired by English king Henry VIII in 1540 and in 1563 was chartered to a group of merchants by Queen Elizabeth for the Atlantic slave trade. Under John Hawkins the *Jesus of Lübeck* made four voyages to West Africa and the West Indies between 1562 and 1568 – embedding in Africans a link between the cruelty of slavery and the name Jesus.

That European form of Jesus enslaved the minds of millions of black people who live today with no future plans as the only hope they expect lies in heaven. In reality there must be a way out of this enslavement, but for many African revolutionaries, Jesus symbolises oppression and servitude. For them, the right solution is to return to the gods their ancestors worshipped. Yet, logic dictates those gods were unable to protect and save the ancestors from European attack as they were weak. Consequently, there is no option personally to trust in something that has revealed its limitations against European powers.

However, the question of Jesus can be dealt with from an individual perspective, since whatever arguments are presented must be based on an acquired knowledge of Jesus, Christian beliefs and personal experience. I believe Jesus has numerous contexts, colours and purposes. Realistically, people create images of religious icons based on their experience of human likeness – skin colour, language and names. Given Christ's heritage and the region in which He lived, the feasibility for Him to be white in the context of European is highly unlikely. He was more likely to resemble the skin tones of the Arabs and Jews living in the Middle East today – tones significantly darker than the traditional representations offered from Europe and delivered to Africans as the divine.

Christ's mission was to set free any captives. A critically important concept to grasp is Jesus was a revolutionary and His message aimed to change the way people thought and the conditions of their lives. The Bible consistently reflects Christ telling His followers the old ways say one thing, but He was relaying new ground rules. He turned the system from working clockwise to anti-clockwise and those who benefited from the injustices and disadvantages of the poor hated His messages. Those unwilling to hear about change killed Christ and they killed 11 of His 12 disciples who were carrying on His revolutionary message.

Today, the mindset that killed Christ and His disciples is the same one programming the minds of their followers, a system of white supremacy. It is the same mindset that presents to the world, particularly black Africans, a fake version of a white Jesus as He is painted by the great artists of Europe. As Africans we need to learn the real truth about Him; the reasons why His contemporaries hated Him. As a people we need a revolution to change society, since it was the same mindset that put Christ on the cross that has embedded our servitude. History is littered with revolutionaries who have lost their lives in a bid to change contemporary society – consider Burkinabé revolutionary and Burkina Faso president, Thomas Sankara; Haitian revolutionary, Toussaint Louverture; American civil rights activist, Martin Luther King Jr; American Muslim minister, Malcolm X; Libyan revolutionary, Muammar Gaddafi and Congolese politician, Patrice Emery Lumumba, as a handful of examples of people who strived to revolutionise a system keeping the masses in servitude for the benefit of the privileged few.

The message Jesus delivered may seem ineffective today given the twisted interpretations passed down the centuries to appease personal ambitions. Jesus was a powerful prophet with a strong message about liberation for those held captive, but today millions of people who have given their lives to Jesus appear powerless. The preachers who have delivered their flock to Jesus have failed to help them follow Him. There is a significant difference between knowing Jesus and following Jesus. The Bible recites numerous examples of demons who knew Jesus bowing down to Him and declaring Him as the son of God. Those scenes play out among many Christians today – they know Jesus; believe He is the son of God; sing and dance for Him, but no-one is ready to follow him. Following Jesus means heeding His words: "Let everyone who wants to be my disciple, deny himself, take his cross and follow me".

The cross symbolises establishing another system to replace the old, outdated one and that is a revolution. For someone to become disciple of Christ, he must turn his back on his old self (deny himself); adopt a revolutionary mindset (take up his cross) and move against white supremacy, a system based on mistreating others based on their skin colour (follow me). Many preachers shy away from this subject, fearful of their credibility and the privilege they enjoy from white supremacists.

Another reason Christians are bound to their current fate has its roots in people substituting faith for knowledge. Misled by preachers, they institute faith when knowledge and understanding are required. The Bible states: "God so loved the world, He gave His only son so whosoever believes in Him may be saved", but it also states: "My people perish for the lack of knowledge, not lack of faith".

Essentially, you need faith to save your life, but you need knowledge and understanding to operate and dominate the earth. That is the salvation of your soul.

God always reveals Himself through His prophets in a particular situation or reality with which people are struggling. He intervenes for His followers. The prophets brought answers or interventions related to the situations people faced in their historical time and space. Even today God's intervention must relate to the context and realities of our problems as black people. What is our reality? We are in servitude and under threat and our situation is getting worse. Our existence remains under threat of extinction until we do something to preserve ourselves. Therefore our most relevant message deals with how to liberate our minds and identity. It's interesting to see many African Christians living in fantasy and alienation, unconcerned about changing their reality or situation, because they have been brainwashed to suffer peacefully and wait for Christ's second coming to give them the good life, they see others living elsewhere in the world.

The second coming will happen and waiting Jesus is the right approach, but, as black people, we must question what kind of Jesus will return. The Jesus who is to come, will not be the one who came two millennia ago. Jesus was a saviour, redeemer and liberator. He completely freed the minds of captives, liberating prisoners. However, the Jesus who will come will be a judge not a liberator. His return will set records straight with the Bible promising He is coming to take with Him those who belong to Him. Those will be the people Jesus the liberator had already freed from servitude. They are people no longer in bondage; people for whom Jesus died; people who follow Jesus rather than submit to the rules of the system; people who do not live under any form of supremacy – white or black – but serve God in self-determination, truth, righteousness and spirit. These are people for whom Jesus died and for whom He is returning. Jesus is not returning for slaves as He has already declared the door open for slaves and it's their responsibility to walk through the door to their self-determination.

Yet, when I look around today, there are numerous people still in slavery, but praying for Jesus the judge to return. Essentially, they are just calling for their own judgement. We need to first seize Christ's original message and free ourselves by walking through the door, then we can confidently call for the judge. Now is the time to seize His message and contextualise it to our conditions to be free. Only when we are free can we expect the judge. Remember people will be judged not only for bad things they did, but also for what they did not do with everything God had given them. Did you receive something from God? Yes.

12
Religion and politics

"Religion is the opium of the masses."
German philosopher, economist and political theorist Karl Marx (1818-1883)

It's important to discuss religion and politics since most people belong to one of these if not both. The changes defining Africa's fate can only happen through these two instruments. No major world religion brought God to Africa, because African people knew God before the Europeans came to Africa. They believed in a higher being or spirituality before the word GOD was created and certainly before Christianity and Islam came into being. Making the same assumption about Judaism is a little more difficult given the Jewish calendar recognises 2019 as the year 5779. This means the major world religions were not new when preached in Africa, as they embodied principles and morals Africans have been doing for eons. In converting Africans to Christianity, the European missionaries took those ideals; interpreted them differently and sold it back to Africans.

Today many African people are stagnated between religion and politics, trapped in an environment where their political understanding of life is diametrically opposite to their religious understanding. People are disconnected from the reality of their lives because of their misunderstanding of religion and politics. They alienate from reality based on their religious hopes when the prospect of their lives reflects a different aspect from their claims.

According to Wikipedia, the word *politics* refers to a set of activities associated with the governance of a country or an area (including a city) and involves making decisions that apply to members of a group. It refers to achieving and exercising positions of governance – organised control over a human community, particularly a state.

The online encyclopaedia defines religion as the belief in and worship of a superhuman controlling power, especially a personal God or gods; a particular system of faith and worship and/or a pursuit or interest followed with great devotion. Dr Neely Fuller Jr. describes religion as "a strong belief backed up by actions". Anything anyone believes strongly and supports through their actions becomes his religion. Understanding this concept requires separating God, spirituality and religion and realising not everything called religion or branded with the names of God or Jesus are godly. The Bible tells us the devil has deceived the world by using the reflection of things people love the most including the names of God and Jesus.

Using these definitions of religion, we can look to the origin of religions in Africa whether Christian or Islam. Comparing the practices accompanying these religions historically with the practices accompanying white supremacy today, the differences are indeterminable – the two practices are one and the same. History reflects the vengeance of Britain naval commander Sir John Hawkins who captured and chained together black people; thrust them into the hold of his ship before crossing the Atlantic Ocean bound for slavery in the West Indies. He accomplished those atrocities in the ship called *Jesus of Lübeck* and commonly referred to as the *Good Jesus*. While England had broken away from the Roman Catholic Church to create the Protestant Church of England by the time Hawkins was plying his transatlantic slave trade. Around 1442 the first slaves were taken out of West Africa. Spain and Portugal had a territorial dispute and the Pope Eugene IV told them to stop fighting among themselves saying that one must take the east and another must take the west. This was a profound statement by the Pope as the leading arbitrator at that time and reflects the sanction which Europeans gave to slavery.

Pope Eugene IV further said: "You are all authorised to reduce into servitude the infidel people, because they are outside of God's grace."

This was the Catholic Church sanctioning the slave trade, finding no contradiction in being Christians and slave traders at the same time. In 1564, Queen Elizabeth I, the Protestant daughter of King Henry VIII and his second wife Anne Boleyn, invested in Hawkins by leasing him the old 700-ton ship *Jesus of Lübeck* along with three smaller ships. Hawkins sailed with his second cousin Sir Francis Drake to the African west coast privateering along the way and, by the time he had departed the African coastline, his ships carried African slaves shackled together in the bowels of his vessels.

History reflects 400 people survived that transatlantic journey to Borburata on the western Venezuelan coast to be traded as slaves. It is in this horrific scenario that Hawkins is remembered as the first English trader to have profited from the Triangle Trade – a triangular transatlantic route connecting England to the west African coast and the eastern American seaboard (in territories today reflected as North and South America) – where traders sold supplies to the colonies ill-supplied by their home countries. In the late 16th century there was significant demand for African slaves in the Spanish colonies of Santo Domingo and Venezuela with Hawkins supplying into the gap.

Today we deal with the same practices, but now the dominant religion is white supremacy. Numerous people, black and white, believe in white supremacy and undertake actions geared towards keeping working efficiently. Dr Neely Fuller Jr says anyone who does not understand racism or white supremacy; what it is and how it functions, means that anything else they understand, can only confuse them. As black Africans how can we believe people who have travelled the world printing and preaching the Bible, but simultaneously build weapons of mass destruction to destroy their enemies? Consider – the Bible is a powerful book based on love and forgiveness to our enemies. Why would someone who believes in the most powerful God feel insecure in their own skin? These are people who have destroyed civilisations and the future of other cultures and people as they have navigated the world. There is no place where European explorers arrived bringing their Christianity and left a legacy of peace and humanity. What can be understood by that reality is they don't believe in the true creator or in Jesus Christ. They use religion, but they don't want to use the substance of religion specifically spirituality. Since black people are the purest people, we believe in its purest form in the manner in which they were taught to us. For the Europeans, it was and still remains, a political game. African American historian, professor and pioneer of pan-African studies John Henrick Clarke draws parallels between what the Arabs have done to Islam and what Europeans have done to Christianity – in both cases the spiritual aspect has been subtracted and the religion transformed into a tool for political opportunism.

How can people use religion? Surely religion is a powerful instrument of transformation if based on the divine principles of love, righteousness and justice? In one sense the world is already embroiled in the biggest religion, namely white supremacy and anything helping our enemy conquer us has to be considered as strong. Maybe their weapons are even stronger than anything in which we have believed before. It is our responsibility to learn how to turn around those strengths to use them to our advantage. The French rapper, Medine wrote: "Faith is a true story told by thieves and liars, when the masses interfere in the author's message the strong become stronger to dominate, now we have been electrocuted by currents of thought, let's protect the faith of itself, do not just make it a tutorial because where man ignites the text, he will eventually burn the people, but the books are quiet, only men give them voice."

13
God's Kingdom

"Instead, desire first and foremost God's Kingdom and God's righteousness and all these things will be given to you as well."
Matthew 6:33.

This verse is the fundamental recommendation of Jesus to His disciple about the kingdom of God. Every one of the prophets before Him had come to their time and place for a mission, specifically to bring back people to God and Christ's mission was no different. The Bible states the creation of earth and humans were God's intention to extend His kingdom from heaven to earth. Man was meant to rule in God's earthly kingdom, but because of sin, death entered the realm and man lost his ability and power to rule. It was under these circumstances Jesus came to earth to restore man.

This chapter tackles the question of the kingdom of God and what men and women should do to live there. The Bible states every creature living in the kingdom of God glorifies Him and the greatest worship and praise God expects from man is to do correctly and proficiently the tasks and duties He gave them. When God created man, He didn't ask him to sing and dance to glorify Him. He gave them a duty – cultivate, dominate, multiply and subdue the earth. In 1 Corinthians 4:20 it states the kingdom of God is not in word, but in power and specifically that power is in the ability to work. The apostle Paul indicates the kingdom of God is not in word, but in working. In the Gospel of Thomas, one of the powerful books omitted from the Bible at the First Council of Nicaea where the European concept of Christianity was fabricated, Jesus told His disciples: "If those who lead you say to you, look God's kingdom is in the sky; then the birds of the sky will precede you. If they say to you, it is in the sea, the fish will precede you. Rather say, God's kingdom is within you and it is outside you".

In Luke 17:20, the Pharisees questioned Jesus about when the kingdom of God would come and He answered: "The kingdom of God does not come with observation, neither shall they say, it is here or there, for behold, the kingdom of God is within you".

The First Council of Nicaea was a council of Christian bishops convened in the Bithynian city of Nicaea (now Iznik, Turkey) by Roman Emperor Constantine I in AD325. This ecumenical council was the first effort to attain consensus in the Church through an assembly representing the whole of Christendom at the time. Hosius of Corduba, historically accepted as one of the papal legates, may have presided over its deliberations.

The council's main accomplishments were settling the Christological issue of the divine nature of God the Son and His relationship to God the Father; constructing the first part of the Nicene Creed, the statement of belief widely used in Christian liturgy; establishing uniform observance of the date of Easter and promulgating early Canon Law.

These two scriptures explain where we should expect the restoration to happen. It is within us – a viewpoint contrary to the one held by many Christians and Muslims today who expect a spectacular kingdom that will turn around everything. This hope might have value and still hold true, but it puts minds to sleep as people wait for God to bring His spectacular kingdom to earth. While we should primarily seek the restoration of God's glory in us, Jesus said: "Seek first the kingdom". Note, He didn't instruct us to *wait* for the kingdom.

By seeking something, you know the thing you seek exists. However, it's not given or presented to you and therefore you have to seek and find it. In the case of the kingdom of God, it is to be found within *you*. This begs the question about how one seeks the kingdom of God within themselves. In Matthew 5: 16 Jesus said: "Let your light shine before people, so they can see your good works and praise your father in heaven".

In this text Jesus explains how one can seek out the kingdom of God – by allowing your light to shine. That light is within everyone regardless of our birthplace and race. It is not even off requiring a switch for it be lit, otherwise Jesus would have instructed us to turn on our lights.

Light has a variety of uses. You can use it to burn people; use it to bring a worm to people and you can use it to brighten the way for others. Christ asks us to use our light for good work, so people will praise our father in heaven. The kingdom of God embodies people praising God and God wanting nothing beyond His glory. The only way you can glorify Him is to follow Christ's recommendations. You may constantly claim to be Christian, but what good works are you doing to get people praising God?

In Matthew 28:19 Jesus orders His disciples to "go and make disciples of all nations". It is this scripture that many evangelists use to preach the gospel, but it is misunderstood. The word *disciple* means student, so Jesus was actually instructing His disciples to teach people from all institutions – politics, education, business. Into those arenas, disciples must teach people about shining their light through good works. Yet, you cannot teach someone unless you have influence over them and you only have influence with position, power, knowledge, skills and sometimes wealth. Let's talk about position and wealth. Position is critical with Jesus saying: "You don't turn on the light to hide it under the table, but position it on the table so it can enlighten the whole house. You are the city built on the top of the high mountain and it can't be hidden".

Yet, there are pastors today who tell people not to enter politics because it's evil, but still pray government officials, dignities and high profile members of the state will be among their congregation. They preach about the importance of people to be happy in poverty, but constantly ask for money to build churches.

It is in this context the message has been given the wrong interpretation and cannot transform people's lives. Those who don't understand the message have narrowed it to only one element – the end of time and paradise are near and hence people must disengage from their current activities to build their lives to have a future in heaven. If we consider the following illustration we can understand what God wants from us. A father sends his son to another city to study, but neither party are excited for the day the child returns, because home is where he belongs and the place to which he can return at any time. However, both father and son are excited about what the son will achieve at school, because that's why he was sent away. Similarly, God sent us into this universe with a mission and is more excited to see us accomplish that mission than praying for heaven. We came from heaven and will return, meaning our importance is in what we do in this world.

In the gospel of Thomas, the disciples asked Jesus when the end would come. Jesus replied: "Have you found the beginning so you are looking for the end?"

Essentially, the end is where the beginning is. Science dictates if you travel earth along a straight horizontal line without deviating, you will return to your starting point. That means the end is always at the beginning; life is cyclic and we finish where we began. Correspondingly, we must first establish our reason for being before talking about the end and heaven. We are here for a reason.

Many religious people believe the Torah, Bible and Quran are the books containing God's word. Yet, the purpose of the word of God is to communicate His will and plans – and that communication may also be through nature. Consider Africans – as people we are biologically more compatible with the African environment because of our darker skin tone and higher levels of melanin and, as a continent, are blessed with fertile soil and an abundance of raw materials, minerals and metals. These factors should sufficient for Africans to understand what God expects from us.

14
Education

"If help and salvation are to come, they can only come from the children, for the children are the makers of men."

Italian physician and educator, Maria Montessori (1870-1952)

We have learnt the value of education and how important is to be educated. I am not willing to discuss how important education can be, but rather the reasons why someone needs education in their life. The African-American historian and Professor, John Henrik Clarke said: "Education has no other purpose but only to make a person the handler of power. It's like someone who studies to play the piano; he develops the power to manipulate the piano and produce the type of music he wants. Essentially powerful people cannot afford to educate the people that they oppress, because once you are truly educated, you will not ask for power. You will take it." The only thing education brings someone is the knowledge required to manage and handle the power within and around them. The word *education* has its roots in educe, defined as bringing out or developing something latent or with potential. That means true education is not about introducing a strange power into someone, but about developing their inherent power. I believe there are two types of education: learning job education and learning self-education.

Learning job teaches you what to do, effectively preparing you to be a creature of circumstance. The learning self teaches you how to do and use, making you the creator of circumstances.

Learning job education prepares people to be a worthy part of someone else's institution. The learning self is the education that teaches people how to master the laws of nature and institutions. Everyone comes into being with potential raw power and meant to build their lives based on their potential. Therefore, the appropriate education has to help someone reach their hidden potential and develop them into a power to master their life nature. The right education develops someone from inside out, not outside in. There are three major educational institutions – family, school and religion.

We get born without language, culture or religion. Those elements come from our family, community, institutions and religion and are the tools we require to develop our potential power and influence others in accomplishing our God-given mission. The family structure is the first institution for our education, but the concept of family is being redefined in modern society with maleness being confused with manhood.

Thereafter follows education through schools, colleges and universities followed by education through churches, mosques, temples and any other places of spiritual transformation.

Family

Education in Africa resembles everything else that has kept Africans in enslavement, yet, as liberated nations, we have decided to retain them. Many African countries still use educational systems designed by the people who oppressed and destroyed the way of life and education systems our forefathers had used. For this reason we had no chance of receiving a quality education and our children are suffering – and will continue to suffer – the same fate unless we redesign the system. Our parents were unable to make us the queens and kings in charge of our destinies because they lived under the oppressive darkness of slavery. They had little to give us, but what they had, they transferred to us. Most keenly that was obedience to the system, since a slave's mind can only reproduce itself mentally. Family forms the basis of every society and is its most important institution. Everywhere you see is a broken society, you will find broken families. It takes a man and a woman to produce a baby, but it takes fatherhood and motherhood to convert those tiny infants into responsible, educated men and women. That is a difficult task in a society where manhood and womanhood have been destroyed by a mentality still dominated by slavery.

Schools

The education system we inherited from Europe has no mandate to create black people as handlers of power, as those in power will not educate another to strip them of their power. We have been brainwashed to study European education and obtain the highest qualification possible to succeed in life. Yet, when you deeply think about how society works, you should be driven to question that reality. People who study hard to obtain qualifications as scientists, philosophers, lawyers or engineers are led by less educated politicians lacking the knowledge and understanding of life and nature. The most interesting part is politicians are led and dictated to by business people who, in some cases, didn't obtain university degrees. That scenario raises the question about why we should endure a long and costly education as the basis for finding employment and succeeding in life when there are worthy examples of business leaders who have created their own employment and jobs for many others in their society without walking the tertiary education path?

Have these people undergone a different form of university study not wrapped up in the European educational system Africa has inherited? If someone can have control over a society's education, can they also dictate the destiny of the future generations? The European education was not structured to bring out the leading qualities within Africans and cannot afford to grant Africa what it needs from education. It is an educational structure that has failed the very people it was meant to be educating – and will continue to do so until we produce African graduates able to find solutions for Africa. The continent cannot continue producing doctorate graduates on the one hand, but still export raw materials to developed nations like China and import manufactured goods made with those same materials. We cannot continue being price takers rather than price fixers.

Many Africans emerging from those long European educational systems have substantial knowledge of English, French and Portuguese

– the languages that conquered Africa – but without knowledge of self and racial esteem. They emerge as strangers to themselves, educated in a philosophy diametrically opposite to African culture, tradition, way of life and civilisation. Sadly, these are the graduates the mass media showcases and presents to society as role models.

Religions

Our last chance for education is via the church, mosque, temple or any other religious institutions. Religion has a mission to transform lives, brought to people and society through education. The skills and knowledge family or institutions have not transferred to people must come from the various religious institutions representing their God or gods. However, too few have taken control of this responsibility. Malcolm X said: "Religions don't incite and they don't excite you, but they only help people suffer peacefully".

Africa has a myriad of churches and mosques, often concentrated in a single street. These institutions should be the real school of reformation for the fallen people; empower and uplift them spiritually, morally, socially and economically. Considering the number of people who have given themselves to religion and the amount of money churches are making, the major challenge facing Africa today is convincing the churches to redirect revenue into activities creating businesses, jobs and agriculture. Yet, churches are big businesses styled for their pastors and families. People have failed in life, so make money by opening a church.

If we want real change in Africa, we must start by changing the way we use institutions including religions. By continuing to use them in the same way as the Europeans did against us, we perpetuate the devilish acts that oppress people in ignorance. However, if we combine our income as God's servants in building banks, creating jobs and producing food, we serve Him. If religious leaders create platforms to collect a percentage of their tithes to create religious-owned banks and similar institutions geared to funding various industries, including agricultural projects in countries struggling under food shortages, society can significantly reduce its criminal and homeless populations. People pray to the most powerful God, but He has allowed His children to beg for jobs from the unbelievers. How can people believe in a God when we have been taught His spirit allows us to discover our hidden secrets, but equally cannot provide an understanding or revelation for generating wealth; creating employment and bringing peace to people who desperately need it?

Surely God is not wrong; Christ is not wrong and going to church is not wrong. Yet, the target of many churches leaders is self-interest over God's interest. A common mistake among Christians is an unwillingness to dominate, if not the planet, at least the part in which they reside. They are more concerned with their survival and their actions area geared to survive rather than to possess or dominate. Anyone merely concerned with his survival lacks education and has no vision for the future.

There is little debate about the importance of university study, but the courses taught must be contextualised to our reality as Africans and we are the only ones who can change the status quo. Yet, while still following the current education system, it is our responsibility to know before choosing a study programme what we can do with the knowledge gained. Don't allow school to interfere with your education.

Parents must understand the rudimentary and most important education their children learn comes from them. We should strive to insert the right philosophy in our children before someone else does. Children learn from what we do and not from what we say. Therefore, the starting point is for parents to learn behaviours that benefit our children. Everyone has two main responsibilities in life – learning and teaching. There are always people within our realm from whom we can draw energy and transform our lives. Equally there are people looking to us for strength and guidance to build and transform their lives. Therefore, be ready to learn and share your knowledge. Connecting with and learning from those within your immediate realm generate opportunities to build your legacy, but be aware of those seeking to sap you from that mission.

15
What is the Way Out for Africans?

"There is nothing like returning to a place that remains unchanged to find the ways in which you yourself have altered."

Former South African president Nelson Mandela (1918-2013)

Proverbs 6:6 instructs: "Go to the ant, you lazy person, observe its ways and grow wise. The ant has no commander, officer, or ruler. Even so it gets its food in summer, gathers its provisions at harvest". The ant gathers its provision during summer to use in winter, because it cannot afford to wander around in winter seeking food.

Change is inevitable. If you don't change, circumstances will change you. Anything in life is subjected to change – seasons and realities. When change happens in society, it always profits some at the expense of others. When the winds of change blow, they come with the energy that creates both creatures and creators of circumstances. Every season comes with a neutral power, but the way seasons affect a person depends on their capacity to anticipate and position themselves to manoeuvre or to be manoeuvred. Two periods are important in everyone's life – the past and the future, because the present is brief. The past is our easiest period, since we have already experienced and learnt from it. The future is a constant question requiring an answer depending on personal perspective. History holds numerous proofs demonstrating Africa was among the greatest civilisations in centuries past, but our duty as African youth today is not to recite the history, but write it so future generations can study it. History is not written in one day, but written daily.

What is the way forward for African people? Most Africans are learning to understand what holds them back, but retain the habits to which they have been introduced. They fear the unknown, specifically the future. Africa has been labelled as having the ability to reflect the world's future, particularly given its population dynamics, but African youths must question their place and role in the future Africa represents. Without analysis on the parts they will play, Africa's future may well be one only incorporating European and Chinese children. African children will be absent from the planning table as our fathers were not represented at the Berlin Conference of 1884-1885. That meeting, organised by German chancellor Otto von Bismarck, convened the General Act of the Berlin Conference formalising the scramble for Africa. It was the process regulating European colonisation and trade in Africa during the New Imperialism period.

Hence, unless Africans do something different for themselves, the way forward for the world will be the way backwards for Africans. My possible future scenario for Africa is a way out rather than a way forward, since we are still trapped in the hulls of modern-day slave ships – the system of white supremacy. There is no way forward inside the current system; only a way out from which we will have the ability to independently discuss a new way forward. The American Muslim minister and human rights activist, Malcolm X said: "Many African leaders tell their people to ask white masters to let them in their house but I'm telling my people to build our own house." In reality many people know what they have to do, but remain on their current trajectory because it is comfortable. People want to believe slavery has ended because there are some black people progressing economically and professionally and thus earning good money. Yet, no black person controls the World Bank or world economy. We study, but don't control education. We use the internet, but don't control the media. Black people are not in charge of anything significant with even our lands not being in our hands. Anything you have but do not use does not belong to you. That reality underpins why Africa's gold and diamond resources are exported as raw materials rather than being beneficiated locally. It is only by adding value to something that its value becomes our own and becomes the means by which to escape poverty and hunger; educate our children and grow our economy. However, we cannot look for a way forward when trapped in a system we don't control as that merely progresses a system designed against us. We must come to terms with our fragility and vulnerability, as everything we possess can be easily stripped away through war or politics. Remember, we only dance to the music others play. Regardless of the wealth we might have in the banks, we are not really guaranteeing promises for the generations who will follow us.

Africa does promise hope and a future for the Africans living here. Globally there are people fighting, thinking and planning that future – I acknowledge giants, South African politician Julias Malema, French-Senegalese writer and social commentator Fatou Diome, Beninese writer, activist and pan-African political leader Kémi Séba, American clinical psychologist Umar Johnson, American minister Louis Farrakhan and Kenyan lawyer Patrick Lumumba. I also count myself Kabala Hardpiece among those people fighting for an African future and thank these great men and women who have dedicated their lives towards reconstructing this continent.

It has been years since different personalities were involved in liberating the African people. Today we still do what we think best for Africa, but base those decisions on guidelines left by those who preceded us in the struggle. We forget times change while the advice remains static. The pre-independence period is significantly different from 2019. Some previous strategies are now irrelevant and that's why the struggle for liberation is not the struggle for reconstruction. Our forefathers fought for the idea of liberation; we are tasked with the fight for the idea of reconstruction. Even though we are not really free today, we have the freedom to think and learn – and our most important task within that realm is the reconstruction of African families. We must carefully study and understand what we have lost to figure out the right way to the true freedom and reconstruction of African families. Only then can we emerge as solid African societies. Installing a manhood or womanhood in someone demands first uninstalling their childhood. Similarly, enforcing slavery first demands its instigators to destroy the enslaved person's ability to self-manage. Slaves cannot be freed by those who enslaved them. They can only provide some privileges or rights and equally as swiftly take them away. Only a slave can abolish slavery. When you consider today's world, you notice none of the excellent rising countries that rise with the help or development programmes from the same powers that previously oppressed them. Consider China, Russia or North Korea and acknowledge their positions will not be easily changed.

What is Africa's way out? Our problems span underdevelopment; a leadership vacuum and corruption. Let's consider underdevelopment. Nature demonstrates anything living can develop and grow naturally. The same can be said for Africa's development – it can be spontaneous once Africa develops and functions under a system compatible to its growth. Currently the Chinese are building infrastructure across the continent, but this is not a measurement of our development. I once arrived in another African country and was over-awed by the beautiful infrastructure and buildings. My initial impression was of a developed country and I had high expectations for its people, but the reality was a shattering surprise as I encountered a society typically undeveloped. Because other people had built their cities, the people still operated under a system structured to prevent their growth. Our solution is for Africans to device an innovative system compatible to our functions and ways of operating. Yet, when operating within a system not conducive to the African way of life, we are inhibited from creating another one unlikely to merely work against us in the same way. Our first step requires slowly negotiating out of the current system so we can discover the way forward for Africa.

Some people believe the unity of the African people is the first solution. This raises the question about a unity under what system? Who among African leaders is ready to be led by another African as the president of the continent? Who can embrace another African language as the common one spoken across the continent? Personally, I don't have the time demanded to unite black people across Africa; my only energy focuses on what I can do and accomplish. Yet, the current setup does not favour African unity. We need another strategy that counteracts the current settings. The reality is it's easier to raise children in a different mentality than change the old slave mentality. The physical borders currently dividing up Africa were imposed by European brigands and should not be the only ones we consider. We have developed psychological borders as a consequence of the physical ones and we view each other with prejudiced eyes, treating our neighbours differently. When we meet another black person, we first identify his or her accent as English or French to peg that person to a geographic location and history and thus determine the treatment they deserve. Everyone has their differences and can be discriminated from another, yet we should set aside our differences to establish a working strategy for Africa's reinvention. All those European countries who met at the Berlin Conference to share the magnificent African cake (as was stated by Belgian King Leopold II) were rivals, but when it was about their common interests, they found no difficulty to come together and define the fate of the continent. In reality we have common problems and a common enemy and we have not been taught to consider our problems collectively, but nationally. We need to focus on an agenda of common targets and set goals capitalising on our different potentials. This will allow different concepts, beliefs and cultures to unite for the benefit of the whole. Consider a national soccer team – the selected players come from different teams, but are united into a national one. As a conglomerate of individual human activities, we compete over power and dominion, yet our only choice is to fight for self-determination.

Our first target is a common African contextualised educational system. This means Africans use African resources and communicate in a common language. Africa exports its natural resources and thus base their economies on primary mineral prices. When those prices decline, we suffer economically and our people suffer by having no employment, food and shelter that translates to poor health, strife and finally no ability to focus on the future as we wholly focus on survival. The outcome creates two potential ways for survival – call on the so-called international investors to create local jobs or abandon our land and emigrate to America, Europe and Asia. This is a reality currently happening in Zimbabwe, Democratic Republic of the Congo, Nigeria and South Africa as only a handful of examples.

Our second target is a defence system aimed at protecting our safety. Anyone who has experienced war fears a repeat. Currently nearly 2000 satellites circle our orbit with 40% owned by the US. Their primary intention was study and communication, but this has shifted into military surveillance. The message appears to be living peacefully demands preparing to fight for your utopia. Yet, Africans expect the angels to plan and protect them when we should be preparing ourselves for any fights. When we consider a common African defence system, we also need a common African currency to pay for that programme.

It is illogical to preserve yourself by building an arsenal of weapons capable of mass destruction, but demand your enemies cannot do the same. The solution lies in finding a lasting world peace – and the irony may be in allowing everyone access to weapons of mass destruction. If everyone has the same power, no-one will attack another by fear of being destroyed.

The third target is free trade. Consider the African agenda for 2063 and the African Continental Free Trade Area signed in Rwanda in 2018 as the largest in the world in terms of participating countries since the formation of the World Trade Organization.

The fourth target is agricultural development that allows Africa to grow its own food and avoid what Burkinabé revolutionary Thomas Sankara commented as Africans consuming what they don't produce and producing what they don't consume.

It is time we stop celebrating when one of our kin is destroyed and remember the African parable: the chicken enjoys seeing a duck boiling, because it doesn't know its turn is coming. Let's develop a common defence underpinned by the knowledge that a threat on one is a threat on all.

Our population is 1.2 billion in Africa with about 50 percent of this population being young (around 25 years old), according to the UNDP and the world Atlas, which makes Africa the youngest continent demographically. Youth stands for energy and the future, which means that we as the African youth are the guarantors and the carriers of the future, so we should get involved today in the architecture of our common destiny which is the only way to secure our particular destinies. The American president Donald Trump during the recent election's campaign said: "I'm standing for America first", at the UN's general assembly in September 2018. He further said in his speech: "Each of us here today is the emissary of a distinct culture, a rich history, and a people bound together by ties of memory, tradition, and the value that make our homelands like nowhere else on earth. That is why America will always choose independence and cooperation over global governance, control, and domination. America is governed by Americans. We reject the ideology of globalism, and we embrace the doctrine of patriotism." This ideological shifting from the US should be an alarm for us Africans to realise that time is up for other people to design a future for us and even protect us. As we are currently witnessing the commercial war between US and China and maybe tomorrow a military war between Russia and US and their allies, we should avoid being collaterally victimised by taking our own position today as African people. None of us can claim to be free or a prototype of our common desire if the rest of us still live in servitude. You can take an egg from a chicken and the chicken remains alive, but if you need a piece of pig, the pig must die. This means if one of us is destroyed, all of us are attacked. Essentially the system doesn't target us based on our nationalities but it targets us based on our race.

16
The Result of Colonialism

All people have their history, and the history of every people is marked by success and failures, victories and defeats from all the adversities these people went through. All people who were defeated by other people, had to struggle for their rise. However, unlike other people's history and struggles, African history is such that people had to struggle, not for their rise or for freedom, but first for their return to the state of a human being since Africans were dehumanised. These were people who were robbed of their true history, minds, cultures, their names and languages, branded with iron like animals and sold. For 400 years they were forbidden to read, to learn, to go in to the churches. Then after 400 years, people were allowed to read books in which all the images were white, they were allowed to go into the churches where God, Jesus and angels were white and the devil was black. Recovering from these conditions, demanded us to work twice and even three times more than other people to obtain the same result. However, today we have done well and are worthy of encouragement through new avenues of light that have shone on us. The rising light of knowledge and understanding means we are consciously concerned about our destiny. Amid realities and conditions not favourable to our dreams and aspirations, there is a need for major changes in African society to facilitate reconstruction efforts. Everyone talks about change; political parties and religious leaders promise change, but desiring change and instituting it are different issues. You only need to desire change to realise the situation is not working for you, but change requires a deep understanding of the existing situation and knowledge about the effects that change will trigger. Change is a process that shifts people from one state to another. Unfortunately, many Africans talk about change, but haven't personally identified the nature of the change they want to bring to Africa. They are unclear about what they wanted changed in Africa.

People living under colonialism yet wanting to change their conditions such that they become the colonisers is not change. Rather they are growing colonialism. The African struggle today demands shifting away from a desire to assimilate the European approach to life and economics and calling it a struggle for change. As Africans we too swiftly follow white principles, policies and approaches – just look at how we have developed our cities. Land may have remained undeveloped or built for years, but white settlement generates houses, potable water and light. Black Africans follow suit and then proudly state they live next door to whites; school their children alongside white children; speak better English and is the only black person in the neighbourhood. Yet, whites, especially white supremacists, don't socialise or even communicate with people of other races. They hide behind their newspapers when travelling on public transport or interacting in public spaces to avoid talking to black people. Yet, if, as a black person, you have money or are smart and talented in a specific arena, they seek you out; they come to profit from you or distract you from constructively changing the conditions affecting your people.

Since white supremacists have realised the influence they have on black minds, they have used it to their advantage to distract black people from instituting any real changes. White supremacists regularly portray their kin engaging in unproductive and stupid activities to attract black people to follow suit and thus deviate them from their main purpose. Since "white" is considered by some black people as the standard of accuracy, purity and civilisation, white supremacists know they can portray 10 white drunkards and produce millions of black drunkards. They can portray 10 whites unnecessarily posting on social media platform Instagram and produce millions of black people spending their days glued to social media platforms and television. I am not dismissing the opportunities for blacks to imitate the behaviour of white people, especially when they copy something that has value, but everything has qualifications and what might be considered good for some is not necessarily good for others. Anything deemed "good" for Africans must constructively contribute to our efforts for changing our reality. We have followed the Europeans in everything they told us was good, but most of those things were not constructive to our struggle for change. Rather they were distractive, obstructive and toxic to our growth.

Anyone wanting change should first identify the problems and the solutions that will provide the appropriate solutions. Nothing needs to be a standard for anyone when it has been adopted from another. Every African country has its unique problems and every African citizen seeks change in the continent, but the questions about change have never been properly addressed. Nigeria faces substantial security challenges fuelled by unemployment. The average Nigerian hopes England will intervene in their lives to introduce the solution. In the DRC people face security, unemployment and a lack of proper infrastructure among others. Yet, when listening to their conversations, the majority expect Belgium to help them. Even campaigning politicians promise to attract international investors to generate jobs, stimulate the economy and change the country. The same promises play out in Zimbabwe, South Africa and other African countries all believing the solutions are not their responsibility to identify and put into action.

If we as Africans want to improve our lot, we shouldn't act like the nations who colonised us. When French-speaking Africans talk about change or improvement, they base their standard on France and Belgium. The same applies to countries colonised by the English and the Portuguese. It appears the standard of intellectualism in Africa is measured by how fluently people speak the languages of those who colonised their land. We speak about change, but seek to become photocopies of those who came to our shores. We easily adopt their names; cherish their languages; practice their cultures and call it civilisation. We have been converted into little British, little French and little Portuguese – and are now slowly turning into little Chinese. We must stop allowing ourselves to be subjected to an identity that is not African and realise any change we adopt must help us retain our roots.

Change is inevitable, but we must be the architects of the change we want. Carefully identify the things we can and do not have to do for change to be effective. Also in bringing about change, protesting and marching on streets is not the solution. Those actions only bring about a temporary solution. It can force a head of state to step down, but it cannot change the system. Tangible change involves people talking among themselves; studying the problems; deciding on the nature of the change they want to bring about and involving themselves in what is needed to make that change possible.

www.ingramcontent.com/pod-product-compliance
Lightning Source LLC
Chambersburg PA
CBHW051258160726
47994CB00003B/1229